Love Unimpaired

By AJ Ireyes

An Impaired Love:

Get Love, Unimpaired.

Table of Contents

AIL

Why love works!

Foreword

This book is going to make you popular, almost too popular, so be careful as you deal with its subject matter. Going into this it may be easy to think this material won't help you get women, that its just not going to happen, but trust me it will and if you act like it isn't it will just make it worse. This book is not written by a pick up artist who went to the bars every night trying to learn how to pick up drunk chicks.

The material you find in this book is written by a guy who met girls at all hours of the day, or night, and went from being a nobody to a local legend. Granted a lot of the time girls were there looking for sex, but more times than not these girls were approached sober and just trying to have a good time. The methods inside this book are complex, but not in practice.

The time it takes for you to think about the material presented within is the time it takes to score with the ladies. Good luck on your journey to legend status, just follow the material and try to keep an open mind.

There are a lot of NLP, Self-help,

hypnotism, and psychology hints in the material- but I assure you that just because this book is presented in more of a study format that doesn't mean you won't be prepared to pick up chicks and to be hit on by hot women.

The real secrets in this book are encoded in the stories of three individuals, but don't worry each story is broken down into its component parts, and afterwards there is good discussion on the underlying principles of why these tactics are so effective- and they are effective.

As of right now you have 'Game'

I was never the awkward kid that
never got girls, at first. At first, I
was the aggressive kid who just took
whatever he wanted and got away with it
just fine. The problem I encountered
was that as my tastes in women grew I
started packing on baggage. Now please
understand I don't mean anything bad by
saying baggage, its just that the more
women I picked up the more guy friends
started to follow along- the problem
was I wasn't a guru and had no time to
even consider that these guys wanted
help with the ladies. I never

considered they wanted help, so what did I do? I mistakenly started taking advice from some so called pick up artists and I transferred this info to the rear, I started packing baggage just like the average pick up artist is bound to do.

The main focus of my energies in teaching you these methods comes from a sort of empathy for my readers. To explain I must remind the reader that I was very popular from the get go, it was just that I quickly got bogged down by the world. The tricks and methods I give here are based a lot on being natural, but more-so on what works in the real world, and how to effectively perform, or out-perform, all of the competition.

When it comes down to what makes a
real pick up artist, or any playboy for
that matter, the secret is just as I
will divulge it. The 90-10 rule
applies- even though the game is 90
percent of just being your own true
alpha self, its the ten percent that
counts. These 10% are what I learned
after getting the girls, and what
eventually led to my picking up the
most beautiful women, women I didn't
even know that flocked to my door.

The Big 3

Have you ever heard the story about the three goats trying to cross over a bridge that has a troll living underneath it? Its a good story and it goes something like a small goat crossed over the bridge, but the troll didn't eat him. A medium sized goat crossed over the bridge, but the troll didn't eat him. And so on the story goes until a big goat tries crossing the troll's bridge and the troll attacks him, but the big goat is strong enough to throw the troll back over the side of the bridge.

Love can be like this to an extent. You might be able to get away with a few little things and you might be able to let others get away with some of the little things, but the big things always get noticed.

If you really want to practice the effects and methods of this book, then you need to realize that a book cannot make up the right conditions necessary for you to get what you want, you have to do this. Nothing in this book is designed to create environments in which you have control- This is what you have to do. You have to go out and do the little things before you can get noticed in a big way. That's what this book is designed to do- Get noticed in a big way!

By getting noticed immediately for your pick up game or your skills with women, you limit yourself to what you'll be able to do when you're really ready. Instead of trying to sleep with women immediately, you need to treat this like the three Billy goats- start small and cross each bridge that you come to, but don't forget to invest in yourself and any possible reputation that might come your way because reputation will be key in getting strangers to offer you their sex.

To turn a phrase, "It's important to always be prepared for success." The preparation you receive in this book is not just tips for you to follow, but actual ways to delve into the worlds you want to be in. I say worlds, but maybe the word 'places' is more apt.

You don't have to go to a bar to pick up women, or a club. Granted a lot of women who want sex frequent these locals, but you don't need that per say. What you do is your business, but with these methods If you try them recklessly, you might end up with multiple women at one time. So, be careful.

What love?

While it's true that I cannot make this book to make you do anything, it is possible in making this book to use techniques on my end that will enhance the way in which you perform the methods on you end. NLP, hypnosis, self-help; all of these things are great but the most effective technique I have ever learned was taught to me in college as I earned my English degree.

This technique promised that by simple writing, and thus a reader, I would be completely able to tap into the psyche of any individual and communicate with the genetic whole of that person. Imagine by using simple commonalities and archetypes, especially certain doctrines and symbols, that you can communicate over the internet, or by pen and paper, between individuals in a way as complex as any geneticist in the laboratory.

The secret is that time is eternal, and for what that's worth, we all have the cave-man-alpha-male living inside us just as much as we have the star-dwelling-future-man waiting for us. Getting to both of these alternate personas is what's important, as well as getting to the opposite sexes.

To become an instant legend in your town, city, state it is important that you do your own research as well. Just for the reason that you have a chance encounter with another living being that also knows these techniques you should know what's behind your new game. Luckily, the first person to use this game was dead a long time ago, so no one person can actually claim it as their own. Why its been kept a secret for so long is anybody's guess, but I'd put my money on the fact that it not only gets sex from women, but it earns love and trust- by the way of perfect 10 sex.

And that's the 10% from the rule we talked about earlier. Its being the perfect lover. The one the women want so bad they talk about when no guys are around. Just don't get a complex after it happens to you, but be ready for one.

If this sounds interesting to you, and is something you really know you want- then just keep reading!

One-Nighter

"From the first time I saw her I knew she was going to be mine." This is what I thought about as he sat next to her on my couch, in my apartment. She was right at home sitting with him on the sofa facing the T.V. as I played v-jay for over an hour. I felt like a clown trying to entertain them just wishing he would leave, but I needed him to be there because I couldn't figure out just how to get her to sleep with me, and I knew he could sleep with her that night.

My plan in bringing him here was to get him to loosen up drinking a few beers, while I stayed sober enough to notice how it was that he got so close to her so fast. It worked of course because five minutes after he arrived she was next to him getting closer and closer with him, just giggling like a schoolgirl and laughing every time he said her name.

After an hour of watching them together while I played cool video after video, I started to feel tired. I could have given up like I usually do and just told them to leave. But what good would that of done because if I did that he was sure to sleep with her that night- and that's what I wanted to do. So instead of telling them I was tired and just giving it up and letting her walk off with him I changed gears. I started playing the same videos over and over. I started playing the videos nobody likes- not even me. And before long his game started to give way.

I had introduced a little bit of awkwardness to the room, and their conversation started to give, which is just what I needed for an opening. I took the insults and dirty looks with a grain of salt and started playing the good videos, the ones we hadn't seen yet, but not before I was sitting in front of the two of them with their sole attention now on me.

You see, they had to take a breath

before commencing the flirting anymore, mostly to spare each other the embarrassment of what had happened on the T.V. Well I took that opportunity to sit down in front of them and start suggesting some of the videos were really awesome, the ones I played while they were too busy staring into each other's eyes. They had no choice but to agree, and here's why:

They didn't know each other well enough to assume they had so much in common so that they could sit together for an hour and cozy up to one another. They needed me in the background making things look great, playing all the latest and greatest videos of their lives so that they could talk, baby talk. Once I made the videos awkward the two of them had to back up, they were feeling awkward to, so I gave myself the chance to come over and sit right in front of the T.V.

Neither of them cared too much about the T.V. though so they had to just sit and wait for something to come up for them to baby talk about. I didn't give them that chance though, instead I sat there and talked about the videos, and not to him either- but to her. She took every word I said about the videos as good as gold for a number of reasons:

1. She had already gave her opinions on most of them to him, but now she was sitting with me and had to

repeat her voice.

2. I knew her better than he did because I had been listening to her and he had only been trying to use a routine to keep the baby talk going.

3. I played the videos so I knew more about them than he ever could have.

After I began a conversation with the girl the night went much more the way I had wanted it. The only problem was now that I had shut down my drunken friend he was turning into a bit of a problem for me. I couldn't get rid of him just yet because he had turned into the entertainment for the night, now that I was done playing v-j.

He copped an attitude pretty quick, so I had to move him to the kitchen with the beer, while I took his seat at the couch, with her. I knew he would have to regroup and try to gain command of his game before returning, which he did but by that time it was too late. You see, I wasn't drinking so I had my wits and finesse when it came to the physical act I laid on my new girlfriend at the couch. He sat on the floor in front of us, but in a matter of minutes he was on his back beer in hand. I had my arm around her, and suggested we move to the bedroom, which we did- we left him lying there, and I told him to let himself out when he was finished laying there. I scored. Not him.

I took her into the bedroom and
the next time I came out of there he
was no longer hanging around. He
apparently got the point and the next
time I spoke with him he wanted to know
what had happened to that beautiful
girl. He asked this thinking I had let
her get away, and thus caused him to
miss his big chance with her, but
that's not what happened as I explained
to him. He couldn't believe it when I
told him what did happen and tried to
put it off as a fluke in his game, but
I know better- I had completely
destroyed his tried and proved game,
one that he had polished off on every
living person he knew. And what did I
do- I used a completely unheard of
technique that caused this girl to love

me, as I will explain in the next
sections.

Recap

    1. How do you say her name? Does
it sound stern and authoritative? Or
does it sound friendly and warming?
Have you ever heard the pick-up lines
that go with a girl's name? Here are a
few you need to get to know.

    -You look like a Cindy?

    -Hey have we met, what's your name
again?

    -God, J----, I know we just met
but it feels like I have known you
forever, like maybe in a past life, or

something.

Do these sound familiar to you?
They should because they're in the
movies, on T.V., and in all the best
literature. Someone always seems to
make a big deal out of a person's name,
but why? The answer is pretty simple,
its because they have to build strong
rapport with the girl as fast as
possible, and saying her name is the
number one way to do this. So its true
what they say about it all being in a
name. Not that that means you need to
know everyone's name before you sleep
with them, but only that if you do
chose to use her name you need to be
100% sure you can say it in a friendly,
comfortable manner.

2. Know your stuff. If you are going to memorize anything that resembles a routine to pick up women, don't waste your time. Use your time wisely and memorize specific facts and popular nuances, so that way when you actually do talk to a women she won't feel like you are wasting her time- like so many others.

Example: You hear a song in a public place while standing next to a group. The hottest female in the group says she loves the song. The alpha male of the group has no choice but to say he too also loves the song. You can now feel safe in saying to the group I know this song its "G--", and by telling them the facts you know you become

instantly more interesting than them-
so much so that they want to be around
you.

3. It wasn't so much that I wanted
to have the best time that night. I
just wanted to sleep with this girl,
not that she was anyone in particular,
just a girl I wanted to sleep with. I
didn't need to be the life of the party
or extremely social, I just needed to
be driven.

It could have happened the other
way around with me letting myself out
of my own apartment, but it didn't
because I was prepared. I knew exactly
what to do and when to do it, so much
more than my pick up artist friend whom
by the way sticks to the numbers, the

game plan, just a little too much for his own good. Playing by the number is the number one way to lose- and that goes for any situation in life.

Drama 101

If you can get a woman's name and use it correctly, in a warm, confident, and friendly manner you are half way there.

If you can use your own specific knowledge of important and relevant things you can get all the way there.

If Love is what you want, all you have to do is find it. It should stick

out in the real world, every
opportunity to find Love, it should be
obvious. All you have to do is to find
the thing, this would preferably be a
women, and learn its name. After that
all you have to do is keep exercising
that name on your tongue and trying it
around new and exciting people and
things.

The real secret is in what you say
and how you say it. You don't need a
routine, but if you want to get good at
using names try reading those books
they sell in the grocery stores that
list all the most popular baby names
and what each name means. This is great
exercise and will pay off the first
time there is a name you recognize and

need to use.

The thing to do in speaking is to match your partner in tone, in timing, and in registry. What I mean is you need to speak at the same volume as her. You can't be too loud all the time, its a turn off that makes it look like you can't hear. You need to keep your attention focused on the moment. Girls love this, and its more fun, so don't try to act.

Pay attention to her and try to keep up, if she is ready for sex that means she's getting excited in a certain way, you need to feed into this and if she starts to laugh or giggle at your jokes then need to stop joking and laugh a little too to show her your still paying attention.

When you talk to her make sure your talking to her. In the first few minutes of any conversation I try to win her over, but as soon as you see this working you need to move your speech and attention away from winning the room to winning her. Move in close and start to speak more directly to and about her, and pay attention- and don't forget her name.

In order to speak to the woman inside the woman, which is the woman you want to speak to, you have to be the man that women want to be with. By releasing your inner alpha-male she must respond in kind, or she's not worth the time. By using this method of

speech and attention you are reaching
her inner woman, that's the one that
wants you, it'll work every time if you
let it.

Flings

"This time its going to be different." This is what I thought as I sat at my best friend's house staring at the posters on his wall. This guy always had a way to really create a great atmosphere around his place. I can't even remember what the poster was of but it was something really cool about drinking and women.

We were sitting around making jokes and sharing stories about girls when I got a call from one of my Ex's friends. She was super- hot and really sweet, so her phone call really got me excited. From what I could tell from her call she was just bored, and since we had never slept together, I was surprised when she wanted me to come over to her place. I was in automatically, but later realized I was only degrading the value of myself by answering to her every whim.

By de-valuing myself I mean I was going in to a set of circumstances that were not prime to pick her up. If we had been somewhere together and she wanted me to leave with her, this would have been fine, but its not what was happening.

I asked my best friend John, owner

of the house we were at, if he wanted to go and visit Meg, the girl who called, and her roommate, and he was not into it. I had to do some real convincing, which was easy because talking to my guy friends is simple, so eventually he decided to come along.

At the girls apartment things went downhill fast. No action whatsoever was going down in my department, but John was into the roommate and made his move by going into her bedroom- leaving me alone with Meg. We sat there with hardly anything to say and the awkward silence was stinging. We really had nothing to talk about because we were both in boredom mode, that's why to this day I simply refuse to go on house

calls to girls who are just hanging
out.

There's a much better way to
approach a woman who wants your
company, and this way actually leads to
sex on behalf of the man daring enough
to try. The trick is to get the girl to
do something, anything. The basic
principle behind this is that she's not
just sitting around, but instead has
some momentum behind her.

I thought the right move was going
to be to get her to her bedroom, but
this was a huge mistake. Once we went
to her bedroom the only change was that
now she was laying on her back talking
and I was sitting on the floor, or the
corner of the bed, listening to her

problems. I was doing better with myself in the living room than I did in the bedroom, but then again the old saying 'out of the frying pan into the fire' was started for a reason.

At this point I couldn't decide what to do so after listening to her problems for half an hour I suggested we see what John was into. He was waiting for us on the sofa of the front room, but Meg's roommate was still lying in bed, apparently in the same mode as her BFF. This is when it came to me to try to build positive momentum and get the girls excited. I had no help from John because he had went straight for the goods back in this girls room, and when she backed him off he got characteristically upset and sat his ass in the living room alone.

I took in John's story with a little bit of pity because he was a self-proclaimed pick up artist, who had great success in the bars and clubs near his house. I couldn't feel too sorry for him as he went into the girl's kitchen and produced a cold beer from the fridge. He suggested we all drink a few and then risk the D.U.I. we might get in driving back to his place. He believed that by getting the girls into his territory he could get them to do anything he liked.

I thought better of his plan and suggested that Meg grab her roommate from her room, before John tried making his move again. Meg retrieved her friend and while they both gave John some of the coldest stares I have ever seen as he stood leaning over the kitchen counter drinking his beer. I told John to hang out and finish off a few more beers while I took the ladies for a walk.

It was the change of atmosphere that they needed- no more distress, no more idle minds, no more problems, and no more John. We found a Pair of swing-sets around back of the girls' apartment complex, and we actually enjoyed using them, taking turns pushing each other. When we had finally cleared our minds and were living in the present, just enjoying each other's company things changed on the spot.

We all became less like animal predators trying to scare each other off, and we became more intimate with each other like we really were friends for life. We went back in to see where John had ended up, and he was about a beer away from passing out on the girl's sofa, he was drowning in self-pity.

The girls and I hardly even noticed the slurs that came out of him as we passed by him to Meg's bedroom where we could all three of us spend some time. And that was it- we brought the positive attitudes with us into the bedroom and ended up having sex until 3 in the morning.

That's right I got the goods and didn't try any of the patented pick up artist moves that John swears by to this day, as he fills his apartment with trophy after trophy from his last night's conquest. I chose to keep my self- motivated and attentive to the women around me and now I have no problem getting sex whenever I want it.

Recap

1. Momentum- You have to have it before sex. Momentum is like Viagra, only its 100% natural. You need a girl to not just be sitting around half the day before she decides to call you for

some action. The wrong way to build momentum is to tire the girl out, doing too much. I tired girl isn't a fun girl, unless she's younger than you, because than she likely has more energy than after you wear out.

Good momentum starts like an hour before the prime time to get her to have sex with you. An hour is enough time for you to get ready for work, to get ready for the big game on T.V., or to unwind after dinner. The momentum you need to build does not come from her watching t.v. all day. If she calls you from her sofa wanting to talk or hang out because she's been stuck to the sofa all day and she's tired of reruns, this is not good.

After a woman has a completely lazy day she is full of bad energy, she's just been building up a bad negative ball of emotion all day, and now she wants to share that with you. If she chose you to be the one to share all her inner turmoil with, you should definitely reassess the situation, because that energy turned to sex is not the kind of sex you want.

2. Atmosphere is something you create. Its not something you should be afraid of, and it is totally under your control, unlike people.

To really get what it means to create atmosphere you need to leave your preconceived notions at the door. Atmosphere doesn't have to be preplanned or set up in your living room, kitchen, or bathroom. It doesn't exist in a restaurant or in the club, as a matter of fact it doesn't exist. And running around looking for it is a mistake- only if you can't find it. Its not really inside you, but that's a good guess too.

All it takes to create positive feelings about a place is an open attitude. Its a lot like the saying 'you can't see the forest through the trees." In the same way its like going into a flower garden and after examining every single flower leaving to see the other gardens in the area without, you guessed 'stopping to smell the roses." The secret is to look at the whole and stay focused on the individual, only not the individuals that make up the whole, but the individual you are- or who your lover is.

3. Keep yourself clean! This means a lot in the real world. A clean person is one who does not allow the clutter in life to fill his rooms or his mind. I cannot stress it enough that living in a way that reflects inner harmony creates situations in the real world that are harmonious. Getting angry, or overly self- confident are two of the biggest mistakes a pick- up artist can make. They lead to trouble and can easily be avoided by a discriminating person.

What it takes to pick up a beautiful woman is an art, a pick up artist needs to know complete mastery over his actions and his surroundings at all times. This is the only true way to make a women believe they are wanted. You can practice for hours picking up women, but never really understand what it means. If your scoring with the girls its because you have mastered something, but what you master is a part of you- it is you.

Drama 201

So, in order to love a woman, or to be her lover, what it really takes is for you to first love yourself. I hear people all the time telling me that they can't love themselves, but then turn around and pick up a woman that feels the same way about themselves. If you really want to hear something messed up then listen to this. The man who picks up the girl that is like him is locked into that relationship, and they deserve each other.

The art of the pick up is to pick-up the girls that are out of your league, or at least the ones you believe to be so. It takes a real dummy to not see that he has learned the wrong material after his relationships end one after another after another. You need to realize that by being a better person you really are offering what every woman wants. You are tapping into the psyche of all women when you become a pick up artist with skills.

By letting women revolve around you and your plans of action you are in essence inviting women to sleep with you, just for fun. And women love to do this as long as there is no detriment to their selves. The way to ensure no harm is done is to tap deep into her inner desire for an alpha male, and then to create the environment in which you are that male.

When you do this to a woman the woman automatically senses that there are no real strings attached outside of the agreement that you share together.

And there isn't either, its all it takes. Be the real world player with class, and create worlds in which her psyche can find fulfillment then you will receive sexual fulfillment together. Its kind of like visiting a fantasy suite in a hotel- without paying the bill.

You are the only one that can create this magic world for her, and she will come to you for it. Not only that but remember how I promised that women that are complete strangers to you will flock to you, well this is why, and this is a powerful technique almost entirely overlooked by 99% of pick up artists too busy with their selves and their conquests back at the super social bar or club.

Relationships

"Sometimes I wish there were three of me." This is what I sometimes think about, but I'm pretty sure a lot of the time that three wouldn't be enough of me. Realistically though one is enough of me, just so long as I can pick up beautiful women, whom will do most of the work.

The first time I met Josie I was working my ass off as usual trying to work my way through college. She was gorgeous and tall, she was it. I had been working at this place near my college campus for almost a year when she got on and I found out she was trying to do the same thing.

I was top of my class at school, but that didn't get me any breaks at work. I worked hard every day with some real work-ethic (that is until Josie started working with me.) I immediately saw the attention she received at work, and I knew that if I landed her with some quality pick up material I could make life a lot easier for the both of us.

The key to working with her was that no matter what she did she always got a break, this included time to talk to guys and boyfriends while she was on the clock. I never got away with slacking off on the clock, so I figured with a little effort I get Josie back to work, only now she'd be doing most of my work.

The boss didn't care what she did, she was too good looking, and I began to talk to her and show her the ropes at work. Giving her the impression that my job was great and that I was really good at it, and hard-working, was easy because all I had to do was watch out for her to start to slack off and talk to other guys and then I would immediately concentrate on whatever it was I was doing only way more hardcore than the task required.

By my concentrating on what I was

doing I was actually giving off the impression that I was having more fun than anyone else. The next time I spoke to Josie, and she was slacking off a little before the end of the day, all I had to do was ask her for a little help at what I was doing to get out of there. She liked talking to me already, and now she had a reason to get physical, which is a good thing- Kino!

Anyway, those late night work sessions escalated pretty quickly and before long she was coming home with me and we were having great sex! The effort I put into showing her things at work paid off double when she now used her spare time at work in doing the tasks I hated doing, and she almost

never spoke to other guys anymore
because she was too busy.

The first time I met Ness I was
stunned. She was the average sorority
girl, but in most of my classes
sorority life was the biggest secret
since Socrates. She was smart and
beautiful, but she was way to quiet.
None of the guys in our classes at the
college new how to approach her, so she
seemed very untouchable.

The only reason she even knew I
existed was I was very vocal in my
classes and I liked to help other
classmates when I had a chance. Ness
didn't need help though because she was
straight A material, the only way to
approach her was to wait, which is a

strong point of mine- patience.

After our classes really started
to move along in the materials we were
responsible for I didn't have much time
to fantasize about what it would be
like to pick up on Ness, so I did what
I did best- I focused on the task at
hand, which happened to be getting an
insane amount of paperwork turned in.

I needed a way to get the smartest
and prettiest girl in class to liven up
a bit so these classes would be
bearable, so I decided to put in some
extra time after class. Gathering my
papers and hanging around after class
was dismissed was a good move because
it reminded me that I wasn't the only
one falling behind.

I quickly moved this taking of a few extra minutes after class to my creating an encounter with Ness. She never hung around after class, but at least I could see which way she was going. I approached her in the same fashion as most beautiful women and didn't even give her a chance to act shy. I used my efforts to make myself look like the cool kid come apart. I shuffled papers as I walked next to her, but as soon as she noticed this I cut the act and concentrated my effort, which had the effect of quickly assembling my papers while moving at her pace, side- by- side with her step. I came together in front of her and she was amazed; she saw what she wanted but never took the time to ask for- me.

It was a long walk that day, but it was nice and sunny outside, so taking her time Ness was relaxed as she walked with me. Before long she had opened up about her life and studies. I used this opportunity not only to sleep with the hottest girl in any of my classes, but also my grades improved as soon as Ness was doing most of the homework.

She never questioned doing my classwork because she knew that I was way too focused on my degree to risk anything crazy. I used concentrated effort to show her it was ok to help, and thus be helped- only I helped her sexually.

From that day on I walked home

with her and she was doing half of the
research I hadn't had time for, but I
found the time for her. Concentrated
effort sounds so boring and difficult
but its really no different than multi-
tasking.

Recap

1. Effort- you got to really be
there in the moment to know what you
are doing. Confidence is a direct
result of sustained effort, and
confidence attracts attention,
especially from women. The saying about
'try, try again." Wasn't meant for
losers, it was meant for those people
that want more confidence in their

daily lives.

Effort is like the moving sky. Sounds strange but hear me out. Effort can't really be trapped up in a bottle, or judged- unless you're referring to energy, but I'm not. What you do with yourself at any given time is what is considered effort. If you put effort into your home life, it gets better at home. If you put effort into your social life, it gets better. So effort isn't any certain thing at all, its just what you do with yourself.

2. Concentration is easier than it sounds. It doesn't have to be like the child's game where you remember pictures. In fact concentration is better left to the individual. It

speaks volumes about ones' character,
which is another good thing that women
love. Showing focus on a task,
concentrating, shows that you are the
caring sort of person, the person other
people want to be around. And no matter
how many times you lose your
concentration you can easily get it
back with a little effort just doing
what you always do- do work!

I need to stress again that
concentrating is not hard. It does not
mean you are remembering facts and
trying to recall them with amazing
accuracy, as some would define it. But
more than that concentrating is the act
of slowing down your actions and
relying solely on past and learned

events and outcomes of a specific
function or whole of that specific act.
Sounds complicated but its really not,
as I'll explain below in the 3 part of
this section.

3. An act of love can be defined
by its outcome; if it is an act of love
than its result must be a desirable
one. You go to the store to buy a t-
shirt; you find a shirt you think you
really love it, so you buy it. Story
ends when you wear that shirt and you
feel love: for the shirt, for your
buying it, and for everyone who sees
you in it because its so cool.

Love should be like a brand, a
certain label of fashion. If you were
to go out shopping and always but the

same label of clothing you would be a model of love. Not only that, but every time you go out as the pick up artist and your wearing your love label, you are essentially letting other people identify with you. Love is never impaired by love itself. You should be wearing a label you love, so that when your life as a pick up artist really picks up momentum you will be identified as a player with game. Sentiment is fashionable, and women will know before and after that you are open for sex if they want it.

Drama 301

Its easy to see how this technique

can be easily applied to the pick up
artist, and so it should be. Because
you have the right to be happy you
should never feel bad about your
methods. People do these things all the
time with zero awareness of what
they're doing, so do you but now you
can easily apply your time to picking
up girls.

Guidelines for this behavior are
so minimal they're hardly worth
mentioning, but here goes anyway.

-In life a lot of times,
especially in the life of a pick up
artist, its dog eat dog- as the saying
goes. Being the alpha male sometimes
means taking things that weren't
initially intended for your pleasure.

Saying this is easy but keeping it unproven is another matter altogether.

Just because you meet a beautiful woman in a perfect situation doesn't mean that she's completely available to you. That's your job in figuring out just who she is, and how available you can get her to be.

The nonsense of it all is that most men before they become pick up artists are aware of the rejection factor. Well I'm here to tell you not to give any mind to this type of thinking. A rejection from a woman simply means that you are not completely giving her the 'go' to please you. Believe it or not you've got the alpha male in you- its just bigger than you want to admit at times.

You are accessing the girl's desire to please you, and by doing so you are accessing her inner alpha female- that's the way that a woman pleases a man. If you give her any doubt about the situation she doesn't know any better than to trust your instinct- that's how females live. Trust yourself to make responsible decisions and the women will trust you as well.

Therefor a rejection is really just your way of telling a girl that sex could be a mistake at this point, this is why sometimes its just better for the pick-up artist to go for a kiss or even a phone number. You already know this - I'm moving on.

Well...

Now you know. You know the secrets
to becoming a perfect lover. Its so
simple is crazy, but so is love. There
is nothing you can't do by following
the instructions contained in this
book, and there likely won't be any
changing this for some time. The stuff
that matters is in having fun while you
become not just another pick up artist.
Bad attitudes don't make this stuff not
work, bad attitudes just make this life
different. You can in theory be the
worst person, and still get away with

being the best possible lover, I've seen it before. What counts is that you are capable of being different and still able to apply this material.

Everyone is different, and I don't expect anyone to be just like me, or to use these methods as I did. You can just do it your way, but the principles of it will still be available to you, no matter what your like or what you're in to. This book is made to transcend race lines, cross borders, be timeless, and its best to follow any information contained within this book with your gut.

Don't forget that living with game means living to its fullest, which means you can't skip out on the other facets of your life. If you start to think that life is just a game than your game will fall apart. You have to understand that the methods, techniques, and results of the pick-up artist are so real that everyone needs to try them once in life just to be fully alive- its human nature.

AIL

As you try more and more of the techniques herein you may find yourself looking for more information, so if that becomes the case the best advice I can give is that I have also written a short series of novels that, while they are not instructional in nature as this material is, they are formatted to be essential living tools. By living tools I mean that the characters and situations contained in the novels are not to be found elsewhere in any other media you may come across. These novels are unique and completely distinct from the secular culture in which the average pick up artist was raised and now thrives, so if you feel the need then go ahead and try them out.

The series name is "An Impaired Love" and can be found online. The materials within them are construed to develop habits exactly similar to the instructional tips found here, but they are formatted to read just as if you were involved in reading any story.

Albeit, in writing these novels I put my best foot forward and designed them to have positive lasting impact in the readers' life, often without any cognizance on the readers part. They're just made for the little voice of conscience that is said to exist. The precept behind them is entirely revolutionary, much like the think and blink tactics of this book, but its harder to explain how to write a novel that is intended to be read as a manual than I care to admit.

There are doubtless other, and by point of view better, books on PUAs, but the other books by the more professional artists out there have not one single gain on you than you already have- except experience, which this book is full of to the top. The methods are the same to a degree, its just up to you to find your own program and to work it from there- this is just to get you moving remember!

Why love works!

Love works in mysterious ways. Have you ever heard that? Well it's true, but what does it mean. To me it has always meant that love works where the eyes can't see. Before you close your eyes and wait for love though, I'd like to offer these alternative approaches:

Love comes when least expected.

Love is a battlefield.

Love is never impaired by love.

It's the third option that I want
to focus on- Love is never impaired by
love.

For this to be true that must mean
that love, any love, is just as strong
as the next. The girl of your dreams,
if this holds true, might just as well
be replaced by the girl next door. The
key is your letting it happen. Allowing
love to open fully and explain the
secrets of your heart is no easy trick,
but with patients it can happen.

I'm not really a mushy or
completely over-sensitive person, I'm
actually quite aggressive, which is

something I'm working on especially in staying patient. But the point is, that love works on whoever it wants in its own special way. There is no love potion, no secret recipe that is all defining. Only are there different ways of viewing the world. If you want to see the world one way, than do it, but it's essential for good game, or being the perfect lover, that you are able to shift gears, or may I call it being open to change.

The only material not presented in this book, in order to keep to its short format and length are on everyday living. But you're already a living breathing person who understands the problems that men and women face in the world today, so I have decided to leave out my own personal experiences.

Accurate portrayal of true love is more difficult than I ever imagined, it's just out there.

www.ingramcontent.com/pod-product-compliance
Lightning Source LLC
Chambersburg PA
CBHW060655030426
42337CB00017B/2631